Fearless

Richard Brignall

James Lorimer & Company, Ltd., Publishers
Toronto

James Lorimer & Company Ltd. acknowledges the support of the Canada Council for the Arts and the Ontario Arts Council for our publishing program.
We acknowledge the financial support of the Government of Canada through the Book Publishing Industry Development Program (BPIDP) for our publishing activities. We acknowledge the Government of Ontario through the Ontario Media Development Corporation's Ontario Book Initiative.

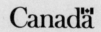

The Canada Council | Le Conseil des Arts
for the Arts | du Canada

ONTARIO ARTS COUNCIL
CONSEIL DES ARTS DE L'ONTARIO

Canadä

Cover design by Meredith Bangay

Library and Archives Canada Cataloguing in Publication

Brignall, Richard
 Fearless : the story of George Chuvalo, Canada's greatest
boxer / Richard Brignall.

(Recordbooks)
ISBN 978-1-55277-436-6 (bound).—ISBN 978-1-55277-435-9 (pbk.)

 1. Chuvalo, George, 1937- —Juvenile literature. 2. Boxers (Sports)—Canada—
Biography—Juvenile literature.

I. Title. II. Series: Recordbooks (Toronto, Ont.)

GV1132.C48B75 2009   j796.83092   C2009-901664-8

James Lorimer & Company Ltd., Publishers   Distributed in the United States by:
317 Adelaide Street West,   Orca Book Publishers
Suite #1002   P.O. Box 468
Toronto, ON   Custer, WA USA
M5V 1P9   98240-0468
www.lorimer.ca

Printed and bound in Canada

Contents

I dedicate this book to all people who found the determination to triumph over adversity in their lives. George Chuvalo's life is an example of this determination. Whether it was in the boxing ring or in his personal life, he always faced adversity head on and tried his best to overcome it.

Prologue

George Chuvalo was known as the boxer who never went down. Even the greatest boxers in the world hit the mat at some point in their careers. But George would never be knocked down, not by anyone.

He started out as the teenager from Toronto who never lost. Reporters said his body, especially his head, was carved from stone. No boxer could hurt him.

George was devoted to boxing from the time he was 18 years old in 1956. He wanted to be the best in the world. Boxing would give him the money and fame he craved.

By 1970, at the age of 33, George was still looking to become champion of the world. He had made some money and gained a little fame. He continued to be the boxer nobody could knock down. Boxer Joe Frazier almost punched an eye out of George's head. George was still standing when that fight ended.

Chuvalo's legend was almost shattered in a match against George Foreman in 1970. Foreman hit Chuvalo with the force of a hammer every time he punched him. He punched until Chuvalo's face went bloody. People wanted the fight to end. But Chuvalo, bloody and bruised, continued to fight. Foreman didn't stop punching. He wanted to be the first to knock down Chuvalo's record.

When the referee eventually stopped

the fight, Chuvalo was standing. He lost the fight, but showed he was fearless in the boxing ring.

Years after his boxing career ended, George Chuvalo was still known as fearless. No matter what he faced, he was never knocked down when the final bell rang.

1 Simple Beginnings

When George Chuvalo climbed into the boxing ring, everyone watched. Fans got excited. They knew he would put up a good fight, win or lose.

During his career George would become a main attraction fighter. His bouts would fill arenas. But it wasn't always that way. His life had very simple beginnings.

George was born in Toronto on September 12, 1937. He grew up in a working-class Toronto neighbourhood known as the Junction. Like many Canadians, his parents came to Canada from another country. His father Stephen came to Canada in 1926 from Croatia, a country in Europe. It took Stephen ten years to save enough money to bring his wife Kata to his new country. They raised two children: George and his sister Zora.

Stephen worked at a slaughterhouse, killing cows for beef. Kata plucked chicken feathers at a poultry plant. They had to work wherever they could. They had a family to support.

George grew up with different dreams than those of the other kids. They wanted to play hockey. He wanted to be a boxer.

"I remember the first time I ever thought about fighting. It was at Morgan's Cigar Store in the Junction on Dundas Street," said George. "I was seven years old, walked into the store, and I saw a magazine called *The Ring*, the bible of boxing. I opened up the boxing bible and fell in love."

He asked his mother for a pair of boxing gloves. "I want to be a fighter," he said. After saving money for two years, she bought him his first pair of gloves.

George's first boxing match took place at the Stanley Barracks in Toronto. He was ten years old and weighed 38.5 kg (85 pounds). But even at that age and weight, George dreamed big. His boxing dream was to become World Heavyweight Champion.

George's first boxing teacher was Sonny Thomson. Sonny ran a gym in a church basement. George's skills grew with his body. At age 14 he weighed 78 kg (172 pounds). A year later in 1952, he weighed 87 kg (192 pounds). At this weight he was considered a heavyweight.

"That's when people started to notice

Weight Divisions

Boxers are split into different weight classes. Boxers face fighters in their own weight class. This means the fighters are evenly matched for a fair fight. Heavyweight is the highest and most popular weight class. Heavyweight fighters weigh more than 90 kg (200 pounds).

me. In those days you didn't see too many 15-year-olds weighing 192 pounds," said George. He became devoted to keeping in shape. He would often wake up in the middle of the night to do push-ups.

His father thought George would eventually lose interest in boxing.

"I remember my father was just waiting for me to get my first nosebleed and then he thought I would quit," George told the *Globe and Mail*. "He didn't think I was tough enough."

George was good in school, but his

interest in studying lessened when he got into boxing. George was determined to make boxing his career.

He fought as an amateur. He didn't earn money, but learned how to box by fighting. Most amateur fights in Toronto took place at the Palace Pier. They were organized by a local promoter named Jack "Deacon" Allen. Allen used these fights as a way to find boxing talent.

The people who watched amateur

Who Sets Up a Boxing Match?

A promoter sets up fights between boxers. Promoters take care of all the details: where the fight will take place and which boxers will fight. They agree on how much each boxer will be paid. A promoter gets money from what people pay to watch the fight. He pays the fighters and covers expenses from these earnings.

fights were excited by George. They were impressed by this teenager who easily defeated older fighters who had been boxing for much longer.

By the age of 17, George was the main-event fighter at the Palace Pier. He was the fighter people paid to see.

The 1955 Canadian Amateur Boxing Championship was held in Regina, Saskatchewan. George, still just 17 years of age, was given money to go compete in the championship. It was his first time fighting outside Toronto.

George made his way to the heavyweight final, where he fought Winnipeg boxer Peter Piper. George didn't punch much during the first round. A minute into the second round he made his move. He hit Piper with a right-and-left punch combination that drove Piper right through the ropes. Piper didn't get up when the referee counted ten. It was a

How a Boxer Wins

Victory happens three ways. 1) In a knockout, the winning boxer knocks down the opponent, who does not get up as the referee counts to ten. 2) Points are awarded by three judges for punches landed, and the boxer with the most points wins. 3) If a boxer beats an opponent badly, the referee can stop the fight to protect the losing fighter's health.

knockout.

George was crowned the 1955 Canadian Amateur Heavyweight champion. The title qualified him to represent Canada at the 1956 Olympic games in Australia. But George had other plans. He wanted to start making money from his fighting, but he could fight at the Olympics only if he stayed an amateur.

"What I knew about the Olympics was what I read in the history books," explained George years later in an interview with journalist Stephen Brunt. "I was picked on May 7, 1955 to go. The Olympics were in November 1956. I couldn't wait that long to turn professional."

After winning the championship George

A young George Chuvalo ready to take his boxing career to the next level.

quit school. He knew that schooling would not help him in the career he had chosen.

George's big entry into the pro boxing scene would be at the annual Jack Dempsey Tournament in Toronto. Dempsey was a former heavyweight champion. He used this tournament to find boxers to manage. The winner would get a trophy, $500, and a possible contract to train under Dempsey.

The Jack Dempsey Tournament was to take place on April 23, 1956. George waited until the day before to enter. He had already made a name for himself and didn't want to frighten the other fighters away.

"Only 18, Chuvalo carries 210 pounds on a six-foot frame and is the hard hitting youngster who has lost only once in 18 amateur fights," wrote the *Globe and Mail*. "Should he continue his success tonight, it'll mean a professional career from now on."

The crowd watching his fight quickly saw that George packed a hard punch in both fists. In only 12 minutes and 36 seconds, George knocked out four boxers. He was the last boxer standing. He earned his first payday as a pro boxer.

"He's the best I've seen since I started these tournaments," Jack Dempsey said to the *Globe and Mail.* "He's two, maybe three years away from any thought of a title shot, but only with the proper handling. I'd like to see him brought along slowly. I'd make sure he isn't over-matched until his confidence is built up."

Toronto boxing fans wanted a hometown champion. George was the best fighter the city had produced in years. The tournament showed that George might be the one.

As a pro, George would have other people to guide his future. He would sign a contract with a manager. He would pay his manager to sign him to fights to build his career. All George wanted to do was box.

"Properly handled, Chuvalo has a chance to go places," wrote the *Globe and Mail*. "He'll need encouragement and solid advice. We hope he gets it."

2 Toronto's New Main Event

A person could easily miss the entrance to the Toronto Athletic Club. Its door was crammed between a cigar store and a restaurant. But this was where Toronto's best fighters trained. To get into the gym, you paid 25 cents to the doorman.

Inside, the smell of sweat hung in the air. Boxers sparred in the practice ring. Others hit punching bags. This place became George Chuvalo's classroom. It was where his new trainer, Tommy

McBeigh, would create a championship fighter.

George trained under the watchful eye of Deacon Allen. Allen had been in Toronto's boxing scene for 45 years. He told people that he was a promoter, not George's manager. No one believed him. They knew Allen was really George's manager, one of his handlers.

Allen owned the gym where George trained. He had organized George's fights at the Palace Pier. Now he would guide his pro career.

George didn't know what it was like to be controlled by other people. He still thought that working hard on his own brought good things. But he knew he had to do what Allen said. George was prepared to do everything needed to succeed as a fighter.

George's first pro fight was against Johnny Arthur, the heavyweight champion

A Boxer's Day

George woke up every day at 5:30 a.m. He ran 6.4 km (4 miles) in High Park. His workout in the gym included aerobics, skipping, shadow boxing, and work on the light and heavy bags. He went to bed at 9:00 each evening.

of South Africa. Arthur was a tough fighter to face. He had been Olympic runner-up for the 1948 Olympics, and had been a pro boxer for eight years.

People thought this was a poor first fight for George. They thought George should have started slowly, fighting less-experienced boxers. Then he could work his way up to tougher fighters, gaining confidence as he won.

George's handlers believed that fighting Arthur was the right way to go. George had to believe it was the correct move too.

"I figure I can beat this guy," said George to the *Toronto Star*. "Sure he's miles ahead of me in experience. But, there's no use fighting bums."

The fight was a part of a night of boxing at Maple Leaf Gardens in Toronto. It was the main event on a boxing card full of other fights. A crowd of 2,500 people came to see how the young hometown fighter would do in his pro debut.

It turned out to be a one-sided fight. After the opening bell, George attacked Arthur with all his strength. George's best weapon was his left hook. He threw hard punches to Arthur's ribs, stomach, and head until something gave.

Kata and Zora Chuvalo were at the fight. George's mother couldn't watch, but sister Zora cheered wildly for her brother.

George didn't disappoint the crowd. All three judges' scorecards gave him seven of eight rounds.

Going to the Judges' Scorecards

There are three judges for a boxing match. Each judge gives the boxers points for punches that connect. The boxer who is better in each round is given more points. If there is no winner by knockout, the match is decided by the judges' scores. To win, a boxer must have the most points on at least two scorecards.

In his second pro fight, George used his brute strength again. It was a first-round knockout against Joe Evans of Cleveland.

With only two victories, it seemed that George had a great future ahead of him.

"I realize I have a chance to make a lot of money," said George to the *Toronto Star*. "I'm really hungry and all set to go."

Deacon Allen said he wanted George to be the youngest man to be World

Heavyweight champion. He made George the Maple Leaf Gardens house fighter. George would always fight in the main event. His handlers also had a four-year plan for George to rise through the boxing ranks. That plan called for a fight a month.

"There are fans here who expect Chuvalo to progress steadily and swiftly to the top of the heavyweight class," wrote Red Smith in the *Globe and Mail*. "Maybe he will, though his popularity will be a handicap if it means he must continue as a main-event attraction while he's learning."

George still had a lot to learn in the boxing ring. His first lesson would be against Howard King. The eight-round fight would take place at Maple Leaf Gardens on October 22, 1956.

King had more than 50 pro fights under his belt. George, now 19 years old, was entering his third pro fight in five months.

In the fight George was out-boxed by

Attack and Defence

Hard punches make a fighter great. An uppercut punch hits an opponent under the chin. Jabs and straight-on punches to the face connect, making eyes swell up. Low punches to the stomach make it hard for an opponent to breathe. A roundhouse punch, the ultimate punch, lands under the eye and can knock out a fighter. Boxers with "glass chins," or unable to take a punch, are knocked out easily. Boxers defend themselves by blocking punches with their hands. They roll their heads to the side so punches do not fully connect. They move around so punches miss their bodies totally.

King, who used his speed and experience. The match went the full eight rounds, with King winning the decision. It was George's first pro defeat.

"There isn't any doubt Chuvalo needs more schooling," reported the *Star*. "But, the equipment is here in both hands."

Over the next ten months George would win six straight fights. But he wasn't ready to face experienced fighters. This became clear when veteran Bob Baker gave him a valuable boxing lesson. Baker was a former top-ten fighter. He had all the experience George would need to become a big-time boxer. It was 1957, and George was 19 years old with a 8-1 record.

Even George's fans were too confident for him. When Baker said to the press that he didn't know who George Chuvalo was, a fan yelled, "He'll find out the name Monday when he's flat on his back and the announcer calls George the winner by knockout."

Baker was favoured to win, based on his experience, and his ability to both punch and take a punch. A victory against Baker could be an important step forward in George's career.

On September 9, 1957, 8,000 people watched the fight at Maple Leaf Gardens.

Baker took the best shots George had to offer. He punched back with some damaging blows. At one point George caught Baker along the ropes. He landed 10 to 15 rocking blows. It looked like Baker was going to be knocked down. But the veteran rolled with the punches. George ran out of steam and Baker continued to punch him. By the end of the fight, George's left eye was swollen closed. His right eye was puffed up, and there were cuts under both eyes. Baker was unmarked.

Baker won by unanimous decision. He also made the hometown boy look bad. A *Toronto Star* headline read, "Realization Comes the Hard Way — Chuvalo Has Much to Learn."

Instead of celebrating after the match, Baker visited Chuvalo's dressing room. He saw a young fighter who needed some words of encouragement.

"You've got nothing to feel bad about," he told Chuvalo. "Only one thing beat you tonight and that was my experience. Don't forget I've had more than 100 fights. You're going to beat a lot of guys and you're going to make a lot of money."

Three days after the fight, George turned 20. He was still a young fighter. He still had time to develop his skills. He just had to keep his career from ending before it really got started.

3 Becoming Canada's Champion

After 11 professional fights, George Chuvalo had a record of nine wins and two losses. His hard work was paying off. By the end of 1957, at the age of 20, he was the number-one contender for the Canadian Boxing Federation Heavyweight title. At that time the title was vacant. If George wanted the title, he would have to fight the number-two contender, James Parker.

But before the title fight, George was

signed to face Alex Miteff from Argentina. Miteff was ranked seventh in the world. It would be George's toughest matchup to date.

"Is Chuvalo ready for this level of opponent?" wondered the *Toronto Star*.

Almost 10,000 people paid to watch the fight at Maple Leaf Gardens. They wanted to see how their hometown boy would do against a world-ranked fighter.

The fight was close at the beginning. But soon Miteff started to get the upper hand. He out-boxed George and won round after round. It looked like George would lose the important fight.

George was behind on points going into the final round. He knew only a knockout could win the fight for him. So he used all the strength he had left. He staggered Miteff against the ropes with a series of blows. After a stunning overhead right, Miteff dropped to the floor. He sprawled outside the ropes with his knees draped over the lower strand. But he got up by the referee's eight count.

The crowd went berserk as George pounded away at Miteff for the rest of the final round. But Miteff's experience as a fighter kept him going, and prevented another knockout for George's record. But George's final-round flurry changed the outcome of the fight. Instead of a loss for George, the fight would end as a draw. Neither fighter won or lost.

A month after the Miteff fight, George gained his first piece of credit. He made

The Bible of Boxing

The Ring was an American boxing magazine. It was first published in 1922 as a boxing and wrestling magazine. Each month they would publish a list ranking the boxers. The list told readers who was a contender for the World title.

The Ring magazine's top-ten ranking list for the World Heavyweight title held by Floyd Patterson.

George finally felt prepared to become Canada's heavyweight champion. A title fight was arranged against James Parker.

After 40 fights, Parker had won 30 matches, with 24 by knockout. But two years before, a World-title fight against Archie Moore had ended badly for Parker. He hadn't fought since. He was coming out of retirement to make some quick money. His bout with Chuvalo was to be his comeback.

On the flip side, Chuvalo was just beginning his career. He was barely 21 years old. After 13 fights, he had 11 victories.

Ten thousand people jammed into Maple Leaf Gardens for the championship bout on September 15, 1958. They came to see an exciting fight. George was the favourite to win.

During the first minutes of the first round, George connected with a left hook to the side of Parker's face. He followed it with an overhead right punch to his nose. Parker tumbled to the floor of the boxing ring.

Parker staggered back up to his feet, but George kept at him. George connected with another left hook. Parker went down for a nine count. Then he slowly got up to keep fighting.

George pounded Parker with rights and lefts. He landed more than 22 punches to Parker's head and body. Parker finally collapsed under the flurry of blows. George won the Canadian Heavyweight title at the referee's count of ten.

The match had taken just two minutes. Parker retired from boxing. He was embarrassed by his effort against George.

George was now looking to expand his

career. Except for ... Bay, George's entire p... taken place in Toronto. H... fighter in his hometown, ... world. To become a conte... the World title, he would need fig... in large cities in the U.S., cities like New York or Chicago.

Chuvalo was signed to fight Pat McMurty at Madison Square Garden in New York City. The event would be on TV across the country. It would be his first chance to show people outside Toronto who George Chuvalo really was.

This was what George had been working toward. A win could put him into a higher level as a fighter. He could make more money fighting. A World-title fight would also be a possibility.

The match was to be an easy win for George. McMurty was supposed to be a weak opponent. But, even though

...ouldn't throw a hard punch, he ...how to throw punches that could win a fight.

George did have the big punch. He just didn't know how to defend himself. He always let the other fighter hit him over and over. These punches didn't hurt him physically. But they did hurt him on the judge's scorecards.

George started the fight strongly. But after two strong rounds he hurt his right hand, his main weapon in the ring. He had to rely on his left hand for the rest of the fight.

With the injury, George got another boxing lesson from an experienced boxer. Repeated punches to George's head didn't hurt him, but made it hard for him to go on. Blood flowed from his nose and he couldn't breathe. There was so much blood on the canvas that both men slipped.

George's family was at the fight.

George's mother never liked that her son was a boxer. She sat with her head bowed. Her eyes were half-closed as her fingers ripped apart a tissue in her lap. Her husband sat beside her. He said nothing during the fight. George's parents could only sit and wait for the match to end.

Most boxing fans thought that George was too young. He had arrived in the big league too soon, with too little experience.

"McMurty knew how to fight. Chuvalo doesn't," wrote *Star* columnist Milt Dunnell. But he still saw hope for George. "McMurty doesn't hit hard enough to ever be a champion of the world. Chuvalo has a punch that will knock down a bull."

McMurty ended up with more points on the judges' scorecards. The sting of defeat went further. George's rank dropped out of the World top-ten.

George quietly returned to Toronto. It

seemed like the end for him. Instead of going back to work training, he went into semi-retirement. He didn't train for ten months. He started to slowly be forgotten.

4 A New Purpose in Life

George Chuvalo's boxing career stalled after his loss to Pat McMurty. He didn't train and wasn't signed to any fights. It was like he quit being a prizefighter.

But he was busy with his own life during that time. On March 31, 1959, he married Lynne Sheppard. They had first met when she was 13 years old, and they had started dating when she was 14. When they got married, George was 21 years old and Lynne was 15.

With marriage, George's life changed. He had to support not only himself, but also his wife and any children they would have. He knew only one way to make money. He planned to start boxing again.

Ten months after the McMurty fight, George went back into training.

He went to a hotel in Hot Spring, Arkansas. It was "the place where Deacon Allen sent George to get back into shape to pick-up the shambles of what once looked like a promising heavyweight boxing career," wrote the *Globe and Mail*.

George's return excited Toronto fight fans. But they wanted the boxer who wanted to be heavyweight champ. They wouldn't put up with more losses to weaker fighters.

George's first splash back in the boxing scene was his first Canadian title defence. His opponent was Yvon "the Flying Fisherman" Durelle, from Baie Ste. Anne,

New Brunswick. Durelle was one of Canada's top boxers of the 1950s. Not only was he the Canadian and British Empire Light Heavyweight champion, but also a top contender for the World title. With this record, he was seen as the favourite to defeat George.

Durelle was 30 years old. He had a record of 98 victories and 22 losses. George, at 22 years of age, had a record of 12 wins, three losses, and one draw.

Ten thousand people attended the fight

Becoming a Contender

Before a boxer can challenge for the World title, they must work their way up by winning fights. It is important to defeat more experienced fighters. If a boxer defeats enough experienced fighters he is considered a contender for the title. They are seen as having the ability to defeat the champion. The boxing champion must fight contenders to retain his title.

at Maple Leaf Gardens on November 17, 1959. They didn't give the expected loud cheer when George entered the ring. Images of a bloody, defeated George were still on their minds. He had to win them back with a strong fight.

George gave the crowd much to cheer about. He knocked down Durelle six times during the match. He did everything to produce a knockout. But Durelle took a lot of punishment. He wouldn't stay down for the ten count. He always got up to continue absorbing George's punches.

It all ended for Durelle in the twelfth and final round. George's mighty right fist knocked Durelle flat on his face. Durelle dropped to the canvas. He turned over and tried to get up, but couldn't. Once the referee counted to ten, Durelle's manager came out to drag his fighter's limp body back to his corner.

George was given a loud cheer as he

was announced the winner.

In people's eyes, George had made an amazing comeback. The last thing they expected was for him to go back into hiding. But it would be almost a year before George fought again.

"Such inactivity simply doesn't make sense for a lad who should be studying his craft," wrote the *Star*. "Everybody involved has wanted Chuvalo to fight more frequently and train steadily — everybody except George himself."

5 A New Contender

George had only three fights between October 1958 and June 1960. As the 1960s started, he planned to get back into boxing.

For his next big fight, George would defend his Canadian Heavyweight title against Montreal's Bob Cleroux. Cleroux was the top contender for the title. But George wanted a warm-up fight. His handlers picked Pete Rademacher as a tune-up for George's title defence.

Rademacher was a well-worn 32-year old boxer on his own comeback. He was a former Olympic champion, and was seen as a tough matchup for George. The fight looked like more than just a warm-up for George. The critics didn't think he had a chance against the more experienced boxer.

In the opening round it was clear that George was in trouble. He didn't have any idea how to oppose Rademacher's well-planned fight. Rademacher didn't have a knockout punch, but he slowly pecked away at George. He got in punches that ran up his point total. Rademacher simply out-boxed George.

George couldn't defend himself against Rademacher's steady attack. He didn't know how to pick away punches for points. George was looking for the knockout.

When the fight ended, it wasn't at all

close. The judges' scorecards decided it. Rademacher won the fight.

"*George Chuvalo's Stock Hits Rock Bottom After Inept Display Against Pete Rademacher*," read the headline in the *Star* the day after the fight.

The result of the "warm-up" fight made boxing fans unsure about George's bout against Cleroux. They didn't think George could defend his title. The Montreal native, like George, was 22 years old. He had a better record: 21 victories, one loss, and one draw. He was ranked tenth in the world by the National Boxing Association and *The Ring* magazine.

George had a lesser record of 13 victories, four losses, and one draw. He was not even on the rankings lists. It had been too long since he had fought more than once in a while.

A defeat to Cleroux might end George's hopes of becoming World champ. And he would never earn the money that went along with that title.

"Now he's been backed to the wall, forced to accept a challenger that could plummet him so deep, he'll never recover," reported the *Star*. "Cleroux could write the final chapter to the sad tale."

The title fight took place on August 17, 1960, at Delorimer Stadium in Montreal. Fifteen thousand people paid to cheer on Cleroux, their hometown boy.

Cleroux came out swinging punches at George. In the early rounds, George landed punches when he could. But Cleroux landed more.

George seemed stronger in the last six rounds of the 12-round fight. He went on the offence as Cleroux slowed. In the final few rounds, George hit Cleroux almost at will. Cleroux just swung wildly. His weak punches didn't even make George blink.

There were no knockdowns during the

fight. Both fighters landed punches that did no more than sting their opponent.

After the match, the fighters waited in their corners to hear the decision. George was calm as the first judge's scorecard was announced, 56–53 in his favour. Then a 56–52 scorecard and a 55–53 scorecard were read out in Cleroux's favour.

Cleroux was the new Canadian Heavyweight champion. The judges' decision brought cheers from the Montreal crowd. But it surprised many reporters at ringside. They felt George had been successful in his title defence.

Rematches

Many championship fights are followed by a rematch. The two boxers in the championship fight are usually popular fighters. If the original bout is exciting to watch, another fight may be set up. It is a good way for boxers to make more money.

Cleroux didn't want a rematch, but he signed a contract to fight one.

In the rematch on November 23, 1960, George boxed like a champion. He was in complete command during the bout. By the third round, Cleroux had taken a series of left hooks to the ribs and two over-the-top rights to the chin. These punches hurt the Montrealer.

Before the match, it was thought that it would be an easy win for Cleroux. As the rematch went on, a Cleroux win looked impossible.

There was no doubt of George's victory this time. He regained the Canadian Heavyweight title. He also regained the respect of the boxing world.

George's success continued in the ring. He won a rematch against Alex Miteff. Then he knocked out Willie Besmanoff by punching him right through the ropes.

His comeback didn't go unnoticed.

When the World rankings were released on May 30, 1961, George was fifth in the world. He was a serious contender for the World Heavyweight title. There was even talk about a title shot against champion Floyd Patterson.

But boxing fans and George's management were looking only at his distant future. They took for granted a rematch with Cleroux or a bout against former British Empire champ Joe Erskine. Surely these would be easy wins for Chuvalo. He would then go on to bigger and better fights that would earn him and his handlers more money.

George's Canadian title defence was held on August 8, 1961, in Montreal. Almost 15,000 people attended the fight. As it turned out, Montreal boxing fans would have a lot to cheer about.

Since his last meeting with Chuvalo, Cleroux had gone to New York City to learn to be a better fighter. He was changed into something George just couldn't beat.

Cleroux would go on to out-fight, out-wrestle, out-punch, and out-pound the title-holder.

George opened the match strongly, winning the first round. He kept it up into the second round — when Cleroux changed up his style. Previously a one-punch fighter, Cleroux started hitting George with both hands. He landed combinations of left- and right-handed punches.

George was slipping further and further behind Cleroux on the judges' scorecards. Cleroux had improved as a fighter. He was able to win back the Canadian title.

Again, Cleroux had guaranteed a rematch. Dates were talked about and agreed upon. But George was not to get another chance. Cleroux failed to go through with a fourth title fight.

The loss ended George's plans to regain the Canadian title. It also dashed his hopes for a World title. He was left trying to save his career from crumbling away to nothing. Winners always fight another day. Losers become unwanted and forgotten.

George had to make a good showing in his next big fight on October 2, 1961, against Joe Erskine. His boxing career depended on it.

The fight against Erskine quickly turned into George's worst. He was booed by the Maple Leaf Gardens crowd after head-butting Erskine during the second and third rounds. By the fifth round, Erskine was winning the fight on the judges' scorecards.

At 1:27 of the fifth round, George was waved to his corner by the referee. That was when he jolted Erskine's head with another head-butt. The referee stopped the

Breaking the Rules

A boxer is given a foul when they break the rules of boxing. This includes punching below the belt, head butting, hitting with any part of the body other than the fist, leaning against the ropes, and hitting the back of an opponent's head. These fouls are divided up into major and minor fouls. A referee can give a boxer a caution for a minor foul. After three cautions a boxer is given a warning. A boxer is given a warning after a major foul. After three warnings a referee will disqualify a boxer.

fight and disqualified George.

Everything George worked for seemed to die with the referee's decision. It was almost like he was knocked out. It looked like it might even knock him out of boxing for good.

George was 24 years old and had boxed as a professional for six years. People said this loss would be the end of his career.

Only pure determination could save George as a boxer.

6 Down, But Not Out

When George Chuvalo was young, he had dreamed he would become the World Heavyweight Champion. He wanted the fame that went along with the title. He wanted to be known as the toughest man in the world.

This young man's dream fuelled his early years as a boxer, from the time he was 18 years old. Six years later his dreams had grown up. He was a husband and a father. To a man with a family, a World

Championship would mean a lot of money. It would mean he would always have enough money to support his family.

After the Erskine fight, these dreams seemed like a fantasy.

George put aside his boxing career to sell used cars. He thought this would be a better way to provide money for his family. But it took him less than a year to find that it was not his kind of job. He had even less money than before he quit boxing. So he planned to return to the ring.

But George decided that his career needed a change in management. He borrowed money to buy out his contract with Deacon Allen. And he had to find a trainer who could shape him into a better fighter. George was ready to gamble what little he owned to return to top boxing form. He wanted a famous boxing teacher named Theodore McWhorter to take him on as a pupil.

After 13 months of not boxing, George had no money and little hope. On November 7, 1962, George left Toronto and went to Detroit where McWhorter taught boxing. If George failed, he'd forget about boxing. That was the promise he made to himself. It would be his last try.

"I had to make some kind of move," George told the *Toronto Star*. "Either that or dismiss boxing from my mind forever. I'd heard that Teddy was the right trainer for the aggressive type of boxer I thought I should be."

Fighters like McMurty had shown people that George wasn't ready to fight experienced fighters. But that was the old George. In Detroit he reinvented himself into a contender. George worked hard to become a better boxer. McWhorter's knowledge and George's new drive rescued his career. It was time to unleash him on the boxing world.

For his comeback, George picked matchups that would get him back into the boxing groove. He won four straight fights. People enjoyed what they saw.

"George Chuvalo, the way he is right now would beat anybody in the world," said Toronto boxing promoter Joey Bagnato to the *Toronto Star*. "He weaves and splays punches, throws combinations from all over the place. The way he was before he'd kill a sparring partner because the only way he could defend himself was to hurt you. Now he'll box anybody."

While George was selling cars, a new list of fighters had come through the ranks. Floyd Patterson was champion for many years until a brute named Sonny Liston came along. He knocked out Patterson in 1962 to win the title.

New on the scene was a young African-American boxer named Cassius Clay.

People, including Clay himself, said that he was future of boxing. "It's not bragging if you can back it up," Clay said. And he did back it up. He quickly became the number-one contender for Liston's crown.

George knew he could rise only so high on his own skill. It would take a large fight

A young Cassius Clay (in white trunks) getting out of the way of a Doug Jones overhead right-handed punch.

The Greatest

Cassius Clay was born on January 17, 1942, in Louisville, Kentucky. He started boxing when he was 11, and worked his way up the amateur ranks. In 1960 he won a gold medal at the Summer Olympics in Rome in the light heavyweight division. He won his first pro fight on October 29, 1960. From 1960 to 1963 he had a record of 19 wins and no losses, with 15 wins by knockout. He was so confident, he could predict the round in which he would win a fight. "I am the greatest," he boasted. "I'm the greatest thing that ever lived." Cassius Clay would eventually change his name. It's a name he still uses today. Can you guess the name by which he became the world's most famous boxer?

against a strong boxer to make his comeback as a contender complete.

That big fight should have been hard to get. George didn't know important people in the boxing world. He had no quick path to a title shot.

"I was depressed, almost crying," said Chuvalo. "I was active as a fighter, but not making much money as a fighter. I had to ration my food, arrange my own training and try to manage myself."

Luck was with George when a big fight landed in his lap. On September 12, 1963, George got an important phone call. Ernie Terrell had pulled out of a fight against Mike DeJohn. George was asked to take his place.

The bout would take place in Louisville, Kentucky. It would be shown on TV across the country. The boxer who won the match would take on young up-and-comer Cassius Clay. The winner of that bout would meet Liston for the title.

This was George's shot at his dreams. He had messed up big chances before. He couldn't do it again.

For his own sake, George had to fight

the greatest fight of his career so far. He went into the fight with an injured left hand. But not even that could slow the Canadian.

A coast-to-coast TV audience watched George pummel DeJohn. He wore DeJohn down with a constant attack to the body.

In the second round George's brute strength left DeJohn draped helpless over the ropes. George cut loose a furious two-handed assault before the referee could separate them. DeJohn slid to the canvas. But instead of counting him out, the referee signalled that DeJohn had been fouled on the ropes.

In the sixth round George cut loose his strongest attack. He sent DeJohn sprawling down to the centre of the ring for a nine count. Later he punched him against the ropes, where DeJohn fell to the canvas once more. Each time, Chuvalo's mighty left hooks to the chin knocked DeJohn down.

"Boy that was a hard fight. I would almost have a heart attack when he got my boy in the corner," said Angelo Dundee, DeJohn's trainer. "He was so strong, could break you in half."

George won the fight, but the win turned out to be too great. His ruthless beating of DeJohn scared Clay. All of a sudden, George didn't look like such a soft-touch to the title-bound Clay.

He would have to wait for another chance to fight Clay.

George's comeback was paying off. After the DeJohn decision, he was ranked ninth in the world.

The George Chuvalo of old was gone. The new George was once again driven to be the World Champ. But there was a final piece still missing from his return as a contender.

7 The Chicken Man

To make his comeback complete, George needed a manager. It was too hard to do it all himself.

In the past George had put his boxing career in the hands of Deacon Allen. From amateur to pro, George trusted Allen as his manager. He saw him as someone who could guide his career to great heights.

But Allen set up fights with the wrong boxers. He didn't get George proper training. Worst of all, Allen tried to push

George's career along too quickly. Through all those years George didn't improve as a boxer as he should have.

By 1964, George wanted it all. He wanted to climb the rankings to get involved in bigger fights. He wanted the larger paydays that would go with them.

He needed a good manager to get this success.

To everybody's surprise, George picked someone who wasn't even in the boxing world. His name was Irving Ungerman. Ungerman knew nothing about managing a pro boxer, but there were two things about him that George wanted. George's new manager believed in him. And he ran a successful business.

Ungerman was known as the Chicken Man. His family owned Royce Ave. Poultry, where George's mother had worked for many years. Ungerman had always shown interest in Kate Chuvalo's son. "Everyday George's mom would come in and all I wanted to talk about was George," said Ungerman.

When her son needed career help, she asked Ungerman. Ungerman agreed to be George's new manager. He wanted George to become World Champion.

"So, I started off with the best of training camps, best of trainers, best of sparring partners. I didn't care what it cost," said Ungerman. "All these things are not normally done unless you are a champion. I set it up prior to him ever being a champion because I knew he was a champ. I felt in my heart he was a world champ."

"He was a saviour," said George of Ungerman.

As a fringe top-ten fighter, George needed a good fight against a high-ranked boxer to get a title shot. George knew who he wanted to box. Ungerman was a

Irv Ungerman's (left) life changed when he started to work with George Chuvalo (right). He went from being a poultry plant manager to being a boxing manager. And George was no chicken.

little nervous with his choice.

"I want one fight, then I want Doug Jones," said George, who knew he could knock down Jones. "Irv started arguing with me saying I cannot beat Doug Jones

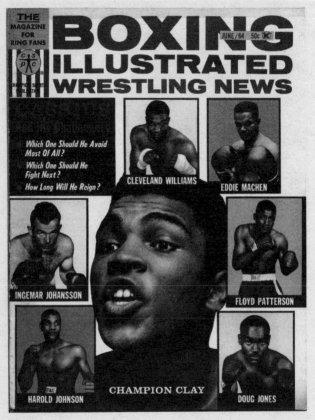

Cassius Clay, "The Louisville Lip," surrounded by all the boxers wanting the heavyweight championship title.

because he almost beat Cassius Clay."

A manager should never doubt his

fighter. But Ungerman had reason to question George's idea. By 1964 Cassius Clay had risen to the top of boxing. He had beat Sonny Liston to become the World Heavyweight Champion. No boxer could come close to beating him, except maybe one. Doug Jones once gave Clay a tough fight. He almost knocked Clay out.

Ungerman followed George's gut feelings and booked the fight for October 2, 1964. It would take place at Madison Square Garden. It was George's first bout there since his big loss to Pat McMurty. Doug Jones was a good fighter from New York. He could box well and land stiff blows. He turned pro in 1958. By the beginning of 1960 he had won 19 straight bouts. He never shied away from other boxers or matches. He was a hard boxer to knock down.

George knew he needed to win this fight. For ten rounds, he and Jones fought

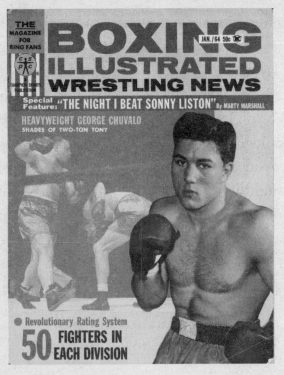

George Chuvalo was becoming a contender that more people wanted to know about. He began to appear on many boxing magazine covers.

hard. Each got punches through the other's defences. As always, George stayed on his feet. Jones could not knock him down as he had knocked down Clay.

The 11th round was the turning point for George. All of a sudden, he landed a solid left to Jones' stomach. It doubled up the New Yorker. As Jones retreated, the Canadian followed up with a hard right that drove him into the ropes. The ropes threw Jones back at George.

George rammed home another right. Down went Jones, but he was up at six. George kept on the attack. The referee finally stopped the fight with Jones

Canadian Champ Once More

The Canadian Heavyweight title was vacant by the time George made his comeback. Montreal's Bob Cleroux had had it stripped from him when he failed to defend it against Chuvalo. Cleroux was also suspended from boxing. In 1964 George defeated Hugh Mercier to regain the Canadian Heavyweight title.

helpless on the ropes. George was declared the winner.

George and Jones traded spots on the World rankings. George was now ranked fourth in the world. This was his highest ranking yet.

Wins against strong fighters lead to even bigger fights. George was now a well-ranked boxer. He was someone people wanted to pay money to see.

George's next fight would top anything else in his new career path. He was signed to fight the former two-time World Heavyweight champion Floyd Patterson.

Hard work and stamina were George's greatest strengths. He would need even more of both to beat Patterson and challenge Clay for the World crown.

8 Fight of the Year

In the winter of 1965 George earned a crack at the big-time after only six months with Ungerman. The bout against Patterson would take place at Madison Square Garden. George had never been in a fight that got so much attention.

"If I beat Patterson I know I would have a title shot," said George. "It's the most important fight in my life in so many ways."

The boxing careers of Floyd Patterson and George Chuvalo were very different.

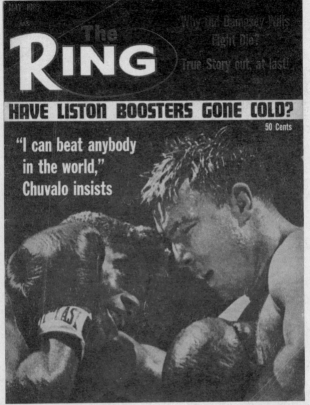

MAY 1965

The RING

Why Did Dempsey Nuts
Fight Die?
True Story out, at last!

HAVE LISTON BOOSTERS GONE COLD?

50 Cents

"I can beat anybody
in the world,"
Chuvalo insists

*The Patterson vs. Chuvalo fight proved to be the best
fight of 1965.* The Ring *magazine called it the
"Fight of the Year."*

George was a fringe contender, while Patterson was a former Olympic and World champion. But in some ways they were equals. Both fighters wanted a title fight against Cassius Clay.

George trained at a Catskill Mountains resort in New York State. He didn't see his family for two months. This was very hard on him.

"I have a wife and four sons and I miss being surrounded by people I love," said George to the *Globe and Mail*. "But when you're away from them it gives you time to think about your mission and to feel meaner for sacrifice."

To stay working, George just had to remember the time in 1962 when his family was living on almost nothing. Now a fight like this could lead to a large payday. His family wouldn't have to worry about money ever again.

"It's had an effect on the children," said

Lynne, George's wife and mother to his four sons, to *Sports Illustrated* magazine. "Many the time I wished he had an ordinary 9 to 5 job, like everybody else. But, he's done it for so many long hard years and the money's just around the corner. It would be silly to quit now."

When George left Toronto, his family gathered at the bus depot to say goodbye. George's mother looked at her son with sadness. It might have been because of his unknown future. It was most likely because she still didn't like that her son was a fighter.

As both fighters trained, interest in the matchup grew. Madison Square Garden was sold out. The day of the match, tickets were being scalped for twice their value.

Patterson was the favourite to win. He had had 45 fights, and won 41. After 39 fights George had only 29 victories.

Everything George had worked for was

People filled the seats of Madison Square Garden to watch the fight. But they would not be sitting by the end of the fight. Instead, they would all be standing and cheering.

on the line. His life came down to this fight.

The New York crowd was electric. Every inch of the building was filled. The sell-out crowd included 290 journalists from eight countries. Back home in Toronto, 13,000 people packed into Maple

Leaf Gardens where the fight was shown on a big screen. They came to cheer on their hometown boy.

The spectators came to see a fight. Little did they know it would become a battle.

"The fight between Chuvalo and Patterson was a war," said Bert Sugar of *Boxing Illustrated* magazine. "George came to battle and Floyd did not take a backward step. For twelve rounds these two men went at it like you haven't seen in a heavyweight fight in years."

Patterson hit George with everything but the ring stool. He slammed George's stomach. He slammed left hooks off his jaw and head. It had no effect on the Canadian. George blinked a couple of times. There were traces of blood in a few places. These were the only signs Patterson wasn't just punching a mighty oak or an old pine tree.

George kept coming at the ex-champ.

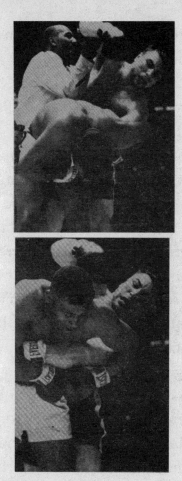

Patterson was a great fighter, but he was no match to Chuvalo's strength in the ring. Here, the referee saves Patterson from more Chuvalo punches.

He fought back with his own style of punishment. He gave Patterson a barrage of body blows that should have caved in his body. Many wondered if Patterson's ribs could take the abuse.

The ex-champ fought a clean fight. But his heavy punches did nothing against George. Patterson hit Chuvalo with a number of smashing rights to the chin. The iron-jawed Canadian never took a backward step.

Patterson realized he couldn't win by knockout. If he won, it would be by his point total.

George thought differently. He was ready to absorb four punches to land one. He knew he couldn't win the points game. He always entered the ring looking for a knockout. It just about happened three times during this fight.

George's best round was the tenth. He stunned Patterson early with a left hook.

In a flurry of his large arms he sent Patterson reeling. It looked like the ex-champ would be knocked to the canvas. But by the end of the round they were both still standing.

George's punches hurt Patterson. After the tenth round Patterson didn't know where he was. He started to walk to the wrong corner, changed course, and then staggered to his own stool.

Throughout the bout the two boxers stood toe-to-toe. Neither fighter backed away. The crowd's cheering became deafening as the rounds started to add up. Former champ Joe Louis and current champ Cassius Clay were excited by the great battle before them.

After ten rounds the fighters still boxed like it was the opening round. Punches to the head seemed to not hurt either fighter. Punishing blows to the body didn't slow them down. At the end of round 12, the final round, the boxers looked like they could go on for more.

George gave the two-time World Champ the toughest battle of his career.

Patterson's manager Dan Florio told the *Globe and Mail*, "The way Patterson fought tonight he would have knocked out anybody he fought, except this guy."

From start to finish, no one in the crowd would bet on the outcome. Without a knockout, the fight would be decided by the judges' scorecards. The two fighters waited in their corners. The people were on their feet. Half the crowd thought Patterson had won. The other half wanted George to win. They thundered their cheers for both fighters.

In the crowd was George's wife Lynne. She had cheered on her husband through the fight. When the judges' decision was read, she cried.

All three judges agreed. Floyd Patterson

was declared the winner.

"George wins by losing that decision, he was that good that night," said Bert Sugar. "Some people are defined by losses. That night George Chuvalo was defined by that loss. He was catapulted up the rankings."

George had won the respect of the New York fight crowd with his brave fight. He was given a standing ovation as he climbed down from the ring and went back to his dressing room. The crowd didn't stop cheering until he was out of sight.

In the dressing room, people hovered around George. At that point, he wanted to talk to just one person.

"Where is my wife?" asked George. "She is probably more heartbroken than I am."

Lynne came into the dressing room and headed straight for George. Tears filled her eyes as she hugged her battered husband. He was bleeding and sweaty, but it didn't matter. They talked to each other softly. She was still crying as she left the room. Then the reporters got their chance to talk with George.

It was not just the crowd that was excited about the fight. Boxing critics and reporters thought it was one of the best fights in years. They voted the Chuvalo/Patterson fight as the 1965 Fight of the Year.

George's boxing that night made him a top contender for the World title. This loss turned out to be a detour, not a dead end.

9 Title Shot

For months before a fight, George was driven from dawn to dusk. He became a machine. His rhythm was polished. His endurance was tested to the breaking point by his trainers.

He trained alone. There was no chance for a life. There was no time to be father to four sons, or husband to his wife.

But giving up so much began to pay off. At 27 years of age, George received his largest purse to date for the Patterson fight. By May 1965, the World Boxing Association ranked him third in the world.

Sonny Liston (left) was no match for Cassius Clay (right). It only took a single punch to knock him out.

Things were looking good for George's title shot. Cassius Clay was fighting a title bout with contender Sonny Liston. If Clay won, Patterson would get a shot at the title. Liston would fight George if he defeated Clay.

People were expecting a great fight between Liston and Clay. They were let down. Clay landed a single punch in the first round. That was all it took. Liston went down like a ton of bricks. He was laid flat on the canvas, knocked out. Clay won. George's World-title dreams were dashed — for then.

Clay might have won the fight, but he was having problems outside the ring. Before the fight he was stripped of the World Boxing Association (WBA) part of the World title. He broke their rules by signing an illegal contract.

By 1965 Clay held only the WBC portion of the World title. The WBA title

> ## Organizing Boxing
> Boxing organizations sponsor championship fights and award title belts. The World Boxing Association (WBA) and World Boxing Council (WBC) are recognized as official organizations.

was won by Ernie Terrell of Chicago.

Clay and Terrell were both looking for a good boxer to fight. Both champs wanted to fight George. But Clay was the fighter George wanted to face. Clay was the most famous athlete in the world. A fight against him meant a larger payday.

"Clay is the one we are after," George told the *Star*, "but who knows how long we will have to wait [for a fight]."

Both Clay and Terrell talked about a fight against Chuvalo. But Terrell was much more serious about a fight against George.

Ungerman feared two things about a

Terrell fight. He was afraid of a hometown decision if George fought Terrell in Chicago. And he feared that if George took a Terrell fight, he might lose his chance against Clay.

George didn't want to lose a chance at either fight. But only one boxer seemed serious about fighting him. He decided to fight Terrell because he was ready to sign a fight contract. George's dream of becoming World Champion could now come true.

"Personally, I'd like to fight with Terrell soon, because I need another fight to keep sharp," said George to the *Star*.

It was eight months after the Patterson bout, and George had a World title fight. If George could defeat Terrell he would have the wealth his family needed. He would also have the fame he had dreamed of since he first laced on a pair of gloves.

In Patterson, George had found a boxer

Canada's First Champion

Canadian Tommy Burns won the World Heavyweight title in 1906. He was the shortest boxer that ever held the title. He was also the only Canadian. He defended the title in 11 bouts around the world. In 1908, he met his match against Jack Johnson. Burns lost the title and Johnson became the first black World Champion. Burns continued to fight until the 1920s. He was knocked out only once — in his final fight. He died in 1955. He is a member of the Canadian Sports Hall of Fame.

who liked to slug it out. That is what he wanted. But Terrell was a different type of fighter. George fought his best at close range. Terrell liked to fight from farther away, using his long arms.

"More than probably Chuvalo would assume his customary manner of staging a fight. He'll go in one direction only — toward his opponent," wrote the *Toronto Star*.

Stronger than Terrell, George would try to herd him into a corner. He could inflict most of his damage there. In the middle of the ring, Terrell would probably run the show.

Close to 13,000 people attended the fight at Maple Leaf Gardens on November 1, 1965. They were expecting a battle like the Patterson fight. George knew he could win a battle. But Terrell did everything he could to stay out of an all-out punching match with George.

George chased Terrell for all 15 rounds. Terrell travelled clockwise around the ring. He would step forward to throw a punch, than return to circling to the left.

It's safe to say Terrell did most of the hitting. They were mostly weak punches. He threw 67 left jabs in the ninth round. He didn't land them all. But a third of those jabs hit the mark, and that got him points.

Terrell's weak punches never hurt George at any point. George kept landing real punches on Terrell's body. He wanted to knock out the champ. But Terrell knew George could knock him out, and never gave George a chance to do it.

Whenever George got close, Terrell grabbed him. The referee separated them and stopped any trouble George would have given Terrell. The only excitement in the fight came when George landed a big punch.

There was no clear winner.

"The bell rang at the end of the 15th round. I go back to my corner and everybody was in my corner. Photographers, reporters, and friends — taking pictures and talking. Everybody was excited," said George. "In my book, photographers are going to go to the winner's corner. Reporters are going to jump in the winner's corner. They're not going to jump in the loser's corner."

With no knockout, the winner was decided by the judges' scorecards. Terrell was declared the winner. The hometown crowd didn't like the outcome. George was deeply disappointed. Most boxing reporters believed George had won the fight. They saw him as the uncrowned champion.

Terrell would go on to meet the winner of the Clay/Patterson fight, on to fame and fortune. George had missed his chance. He was left to pick up the pieces of his career.

Clay eventually knocked out Patterson, leading to a Terrell/Clay fight. George's future was cloudy. He had had his chance at the World title. Now he had to look for another shot.

10 Chasing Ali

The 1960s were a time of turmoil for the United States. The country was in a war in Vietnam. The fight for civil rights sometimes turned into race riots that made cities across the country into war zones. People were divided by these events.

The war was a hot topic. Not all people thought that the U.S. should be fighting in Vietnam. And the American government had started the draft, sending into war young men who had not signed up to

Muhammad Ali was in his prime by 1966. At this time he was considered one of the greatest boxers in the history of the sport.

fight. In the U.S., African-Americans rose up in the streets looking for equal rights. They were led by great men like Martin Luther King Jr. They were resisted by white Americans who believed they didn't deserve any rights.

Great White Hopes

Due to racist beliefs, some people did not think an African-American should be heavyweight champion of the world. They wanted a white fighter to hold this title. They looked for a white boxer to defeat the African-American champ. This fighter would be their Great White Hope at winning back the title from a black man.

In the middle of all this was boxing's heavyweight champion of the world, Cassius Clay.

Among all this change, Clay became a Muslim. The group he was part of, the Nation of Islam, sometimes took quite a violent approach in gaining equal rights for African-Americans. Their leader, Elijah Muhammad, renamed the boxer Muhammad Ali.

"Cassius Clay is a slave name, I didn't choose it and I didn't want it," said the boxer. "I am Muhammad Ali, a free name — it means 'beloved of God' — and I insist people use it when speaking to me and of me."

Originally Ali was not eligible for the army draft. As the war went on, this changed. The government needed more soldiers to fight in Vietnam. When Ali was drafted into the army, he refused to go.

Ali didn't want to fight in a war he didn't believe in. He argued that the government should not be fighting in Vietnam. The government fought Ali in the courts over his refusal to join.

The government was against Muhammad Ali. Most people were against him. All he had was boxing.

"Ali felt the sting of being a social [exile] in so many ways," George Chuvalo said in an interview with Stephen Brunt. "Today the man's an icon. Today the man's revered. Today the man's the most

The Colour Barrier

Sam Langford was an African-Canadian boxer born in Weymouth, Nova Scotia, on February 12, 1883. He moved to Boston as a teenager to make his fortune. It was there he learned to box. He fought and beat some of the best boxers in the world. Because he was a black boxer he was never allowed to fight for a World Championship. He was considered the best boxer to have never won a World title. He retired at age 43 after about 300 fights. He died in 1956. He is a member of the International Boxing Hall of Fame and the Canadian Sports Hall of Fame.

recognized face on earth. And they love him, but he wasn't loved then. Far from it. People hated him."

After his victory over Patterson, Ali was preparing to fight WBA champion Ernie Terrell. This would bring both World Heavyweight titles into one. It was going to be the biggest fight of 1966.

On the side, Ali told George to keep winning so that they would meet in a title match. But George's hope of a big-money fight suffered a setback. He lost to unranked Argentine boxer Eduardo Coletti. This loss hurt his plans.

For years George had wanted a match against British Empire Champion Henry Cooper. Finally, Cooper was almost ready to fight George. They both saw it as a way to get to fight Ali. But that was before the Chuvalo loss to Coletti.

"We're no longer interested in Chuvalo," said Jim Wicks, Cooper's manager. "What do we need with Chuvalo now? We want to go forward, not back."

George's career started a slow downward spiral. His world ranking dropped from third to tenth. Plans for big fights slipped away as he lost to lesser boxers. The image of the tough boxer, which he had made fighting Patterson, started to fade.

Plans for the Ali/Terrell fight were also facing problems. The fight was turned down in Louisville, Chicago, New York, Philadelphia, and Montreal. No one wanted to host it. It had nothing to do with boxing, but was because both players were seen as trouble: Ali's religion and refusal to join the army; and Terrell's connections to organized crime.

The fight finally found a home in Toronto at Maple Leaf Gardens. But now there was an even bigger problem to deal with. Terrell pulled out of the fight less than a month before it was to take place. The call went out for someone to take his place, so that the fight could be saved.

George was all of a sudden back in the spotlight. He was sitting in his manager's office when the fight promoter phoned. George and his manager listened as he asked if George wanted to fight Ali.

"The immediate horizon didn't look good for me," said George, who would only have 17 days to train for the fight. "It was going to be a while before I got another crack."

George could not turn down the chance to finally fight Ali, especially in his hometown.

"I've been in the fight game now for ten years, so this is the big one for me," George said in a CBC interview. "It's more or less now or never."

Ali was usually loud and confident. When going into a fight he would say things like, "If you ever dream of beating me you'd better wake up and apologize." But, now he was a different man. He was quiet before the Chuvalo fight. Being in the spotlight for all the wrong reasons really hurt the champ. He got away from it all and trained for the fight in Canada. He found the people there different from the

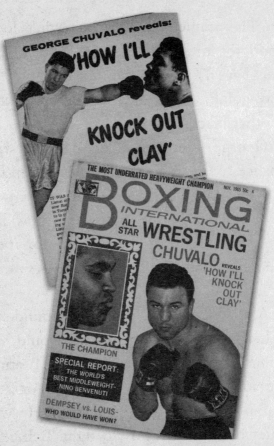

Before the fight even happened, Chuvalo was trying to tell people he could defeat Ali. He said how he could do it in various magazine articles. It would be the biggest fight of his career.

people back in the United States. He was humbled by the Canadians.

"The people here in Canada are nice. Honestly, I am not saying this because I am here. I am not that type of person who says things they don't mean," said Ali in a CBC interview. "I am known for it. I have never been treated so nice in my life. I have no people making wise cracks, everybody is friendly — the children, the waiters, hotel managers, policemen — everybody is as nice as they could be. A lot different than from where I came from."

But when the fighters got into the ring, Canadians would be cheering for their hometown boxer.

Critics had a lot to say about the mismatch. They said Ali would easily knock out Chuvalo, even though George had never been knocked down. They told people not to come to the fight, to save their money, because it would end horribly.

Memorable Muhammad Ali Quotes:

Muhammad Ali was known for his boxing abilities in the ring and his loud mouth out of it. He said many things during interviews, include the exact round he would defeat an opponent. Some of his most memorable quotes are:

- "Float like a butterfly. Sting like a bee. Your hands can't hit what your eyes can't see."
- "I am the greatest. I'm the greatest thing that ever lived."
- "I'm so fast that last night I turned off the light switch in my hotel room and was back in bed before the room was dark."

George could easily make a fool of himself against the world's greatest boxer. He knew that. His supporters knew that too, because it had happened before. But there was a chance that this fight would lift George to legendary status.

11 A Legend is Born

Could George Chuvalo rise to the moment? That was what people asked about the fight. He was going into the ring with the greatest fighter of the time. George was the underdog. But every underdog has a chance when the opening bell rings.

On the night of March 22, 1966, Maple Leaf Gardens was packed with 14,000 boxing fans. George would go on to show everyone that he had a better right to be there than either Patterson or Liston. He would go on to silence all his critics.

The fight began with Ali striking first. He danced around George, hitting him with left- and right-handed punches. Ali hit George with every punch he had. But George was not brought down or staggered.

At one point George pummelled Ali's body with powerful right-handed punches.

"Chuvalo roughed up Clay on the inside … 1,2,3,4, … 9,10,11,12 right-hand punches to the body," said excited radio announcer Dean Dunphy.

At the end of the first round Dunphy proclaimed proudly, "Chuvalo is doing much better than they thought he would."

The more George got punched, the stronger he became. Ali would hit him with his best shots and he would take another step forward. Round after round, bell after bell, George was still on his feet.

Ali knew he was in a tough fight.

"In my own mind I said I couldn't be hurt. A crazy part of me felt indestructible," said George.

Ali had to absorb George's best punches. At one point Ali's trainer Angelo Dundee yelled to his fighter to quit playing around. Ali responded that he wasn't. Before this bout Ali had won so easily that no one knew how much punishment he could take.

George accepted Ali's best punches without flinching. He kept coming straight ahead, flailing away until it seemed that there was no way he could go on. But his pace never let up.

"This was the old-style fight," said *New York Times* journalist Robert Lipsyte. "Chuvalo was the honest worker. He comes to fight. He wasn't scared. He wasn't cocky. He wasn't over-confident. He was willing to take a lot of punishment for the opportunity to give some."

As the fight progressed, Ali did everything he could to knock George out. But he just couldn't bring him down.

"Some of us had said that this Canadian should have been selling peanuts in the aisles rather than throwing punches in the ring. We were wrong," wrote the *New York Times*. "Cassius Clay has never been given a harder, more bruising fight."

By the start of the fifteenth and final round, George was swollen and bleeding. His arms hung from his shoulders. Ali kept at him. Even then, George stepped forward.

Dean Dunphy said what everybody was thinking: "How many would have thought it would go this far?"

Up until this final round, George was behind in points. He knew he had to knock Ali out to win. He had three minutes to do it.

Midway through the round George exploded. He landed four vicious lefts to Ali's jaw before hitting the champ with a wicked right to his head. For the first time in the fight, Ali was in trouble.

"Chuvalo may have hurt Clay? Chuvalo may have hurt Clay," screamed Dunphy over the radio.

The crowd rose to its feet as their hero went in for the kill. But George didn't have time to put away the champ. The bell rang to end the fight.

Ali won by unanimous decision.

"The judges voted for Ali, but he had to be taken to the hospital afterwards while I went dancing with my wife," said George.

George might have lost, but he gained respect and a new group of fans. Two of his newest fans were in the other corner — Muhammad Ali and his trainer Angelo Dundee.

"He's the toughest guy I ever fought,"

said Ali after the fight. "I kept saying he was tough — tougher than Liston, tougher than Patterson, tougher than Terrell — but people thought I was just trying to build up the gate. Now you know I was right."

"Chuvalo made the greatest fight of his life," said Dundee. "People ought to be proud of this man. I was, and I was in the other guy's corner."

That one fight made George a Canadian legend. He had fought the greatest boxer of all time. Clay couldn't knock the Canadian down. Even though George lost, he came out of this fight a winner.

"To me it's kind of a negative," said George in an interview with journalist Stephen Brunt years later. "I lost the fight. So people see me and they say, 'Oh George, you went the distance with Muhammad Ali.' I say, 'No, he went the distance with me!'"

George had gone pro before he had a

chance to fight at the Olympics. But the fight against Ali let him fight for his country in a different way. "In a crazy kind of way it made Canadians feel good," said George. When I see people and they talk about the fight, I hear them say it made them feel good, kind of proud. I made my fellow Canadians feel proud about being Canadian. And that part makes me feel good, made me feel nice. I can feel proud of that part. I can feel happy about it."

12 The Knockout Punch

Between 1965 and 1966 George fought three of boxing's biggest fighters. They were great fights, even though he lost all of them. To keep getting these big-time fights he had to win the lesser ones.

Three months after the Ali fight, George fought Oscar Bonavena at Madison Square Garden. Bonavena staggered George at one point in the bout. The fight went the full ten rounds, with Bonavena getting the decision. At age 28,

George was starting to fall in the rankings.

"I'll take a holiday. After that I don't know," George told the *Star* about his future in boxing.

But George did fight again. He put together 13 victories after the Ali fight in 1966. But they were against weak fighters. George was working his way back to bigger paydays against contenders.

The boxing world turned upside down in 1967. Muhammad Ali was stripped of his World Heavyweight crown. For the next three years, instead of fighting in a ring, the great boxer was in a courtroom fighting for his rights.

It was decided that the top contenders would fight for the title that was taken away from Ali. George was included in these fights. He would face Joe Frazier.

It was George's fifth fight at Madison Square Garden. He went into the fight ranked tenth in the world with a 46-13-2 record.

It was another all-or-nothing fight. Once again, a win would mean a chance at the World title and larger paydays. A loss would push him farther away.

"Fight observers are classifying this one as Chuvalo's last big chance, the one that means everything, the crossroads, the one, etc," said Jack Meek in the *Globe and Mail*. "They're not close enough to George to realize that every fight in his career has been some sort of intersection."

Frazier was the 1964 Olympic champion. He had never lost in 16 pro fights. Some said he was the best boxer since Ali turned pro. Others thought he might be better than Ali.

Almost 14,000 watched the fight on July 19, 1967. They all expected a war. It turned into a one-sided battle.

By the second round, George's face was smeared with blood as punch after punch banged into the right side of his head. Between the second and third round, his face turned purple.

The third round turned out to be his best round. He had Frazier cornered on the ropes, pinned by punches. But then George slowed up. He gave Frazier the chance to escape from his punches.

George was hit again and again by Frazier's fast left hook. That quickly led to swelling and cuts on George's face. He was bleeding so badly the referee stopped the fight after only four rounds.

It was later learned that George's eye had been injured before the fight. After the first punch, that eye swelled up. Bleeding in the area forced the eyeball forward. It stuck out of the socket 2 cm (3/4 inch). Frazier's punches then drove the eye down inside George's head through the optic floor.

George needed surgery to fix the eye.

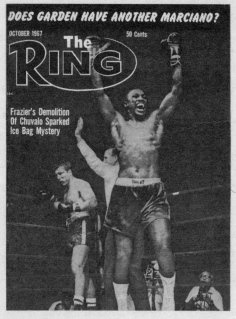

This magazine cover shows Chuvalo was barely standing at the end of the fight against Joe Frazier. Frazier would eventually become the heavyweight champion of the world.

Plastic and silicone would hold the eye in place from that point on.

After the surgery, George couldn't box until he healed. He had to decide if he wanted to fight again at that point. Even his manager didn't know if George could make another comeback.

During George's recovery, Ungerman bought a restaurant in Toronto. He got it for George as a new career. George would be the host and the person everyone came to see. The business was renamed George Chuvalo's Caravan.

The new job let George make a steady paycheque. He would have to work 16-hour days. It took his mind off the fight game. It looked like he might not return to the ring.

But George would be lured back into the world of boxing. The Canadian Boxing Federation said he had to defend his Canadian title. If he didn't, they would strip it from him.

"I didn't defend my title for years and then I get an eye injury and all of a sudden there's 14,000 vultures around me,"

George told the *Globe and Mail*.

What also pulled him back to the boxing ring were the big purses fighters were earning.

In 1968, at 30 years of age, George re-entered the ring. He defeated Jean-Claude Roy to retain the Canadian title. Then he went looking for some of those big paydays.

His first big opponent was Manual Ramos. Ramos was the Mexican champion who'd beaten Ernie Terrell. He had knocked down Joe Frazier before Frazier stopped him. George knocked out Ramos in the fifth round. It was George's 52nd career win.

George was again seen as a contender. He won six straight fights. Ex-champ Sonny Liston and contender Buster Mathis wanted to fight the Canadian.

"Chuvalo was back in demand," wrote the *Toronto Star*. "He has long been on the fringe of the fight game's top echelon, always maddeningly close to grabbing the glory, but always falling short. He's been tough, durable, always certain to bring a good fight."

After a loss to Buster Mathis in his 70th pro fight, George signed to fight Jerry Quary. Quary was ranked third in the world and had dodged George in the past.

More than 9,000 people were at the December 12, 1967, fight at Madison Square Garden. Quary was the clear favourite to win. People thought that George's best fights were behind him.

Quary started strong, rattling combinations and crushing left hooks into George. For most of the fight Quary hit him almost at will. For a time it seemed George might get knocked off his feet for the first time in his 12-year career.

George's offence came to life in the third round when he nailed Quary with a hard left hook. Quary came back in the fourth round. George's eye was hit so much it began to swell and close by the fifth round.

Quary was winning the fight. The doctor almost ended it after the sixth round because George's eye was nothing but a slit. He couldn't see Quary's snappy left hooks coming.

By the start of the seventh round George was losing on two of the judges' scorecards and tied on the other. He could barely see out of his right eye.

But he needed only one eye to win. As the seventh round closed Quary made a mistake and dropped his right hand. George saw this. He whipped a left hook that landed flush on Quary's right temple. Quary wobbled slightly and went down. He was on one knee at the count of three. But he didn't get up as the referee shouted ten.

Ending Up Punch Drunk

Jerry "The Bellflower Bomber" Quary was a top contender for most of his career. He had a 53-9-4 record and was inducted into the World Boxing Hall of Fame. Like many boxers, later in life he was affected by shrinking of the brain from repeated blows to the head. Before he died he was unable to feed or dress himself.

There was only one second remaining in the round. The crowd was stunned. George was declared the winner by knockout. He celebrated by bouncing around the ring like a kangaroo.

Chuvalo had good reason to celebrate. A year before, his eye had been almost knocked out of its socket. His future had been uncertain. He had gone on to defeat the highest-ranked boxer in his career. He was back to large paydays against contenders.

13 Punching Bag

A lot of fighters don't get knocked down for many fights at the start of their careers. It makes them sound tougher than they really are. But they always meet somebody who can knock them down.

At the start of George's career, it was just an interesting fact. He was never knocked down as a pro or amateur. As the years went by, that reputation started to grow. It became a part of who George Chuvalo was. The strongest fighters in the world couldn't put him down.

As time went on, it became an identity George didn't want.

"It's such a negative thing," he said. "So I've never been knocked out. So what? Often it makes me feel I'm nothing but an oversized punching bag. It's not an accomplishment."

George even thought about it when he was fighting. "I remember in the Bonavena fight I lost my balance and skidded back. I heard the crowd drawing in their breath in anticipation. Then it raced through my mind that if I stumbled back and went down, my record would be gone. I thought, I'm not going down, I won't let it happen. And it didn't. It's just one of those things. It's a funny pride and it grew without my realizing it."

The Quary fight was a high point in his career. George had won when everyone in the boxing world said he couldn't. That fight led to fights against other top contenders. He was ranked third in the world at the start of 1970.

But it would be the start of the slow decline of George as a boxer.

George's career turned in a main-event fight against George Foreman on August 4, 1970, at Madison Square Garden. Foreman, Olympic champion and future heavyweight champ, was undefeated after 21 fights. Chuvalo had a record of 59-12-2.

Foreman pounded on Chuvalo from the opening bell. Chuvalo could do nothing to stop the young boxer.

As the fight went on, blood dribbled from Chuvalo's mouth. His eyes were glazed over. His hands were only half-raised, unable to defend him against Foreman's punches. Chuvalo was about to go down with every punch that Foreman threw. Every one of those punches held all the power Foreman could put behind them. They were opposed only by Chuvalo's ability to take them.

The beginning of the end came a minute into the third round. Foreman crashed his left fist against Chuvalo's chin. It seemed that George might go down. Unlike many young fighters, Foreman did not step back to admire his work. He followed right up with lefts and rights that drove Chuvalo's helpless body reeling around the ring.

Foreman was landing punches at the rate of about one per second. He kept this attack going for a full 40 seconds.

Chuvalo's manager Ungerman couldn't watch any more. He ran up to the ring, yelling at the referee to stop the fight. Referee Arthur Mercante didn't hear him. The fight went on. Foreman kept punching Chuvalo.

Lynne Chuvalo couldn't watch her

husband punched bloody. She was also yelling for the referee to stop the fight.

Chuvalo was finally saved. Referee Mercante stepped between the fighters. He signalled that it was all over. Foreman won the fight at 1:41 of the third round.

Even a beating that brutal didn't stop George Chuvalo. He kept boxing because he was making money doing it. Against Foreman he was paid $50,000. In his 85th professional fight, at 34 years of age, Chuvalo fought former champ Jimmy Ellis. Even though George lost, he was paid $43,000.

His biggest payday would come against his greatest opponent.

Muhammad Ali was back in boxing in 1970. By May 1, 1972, at 30 years of age, he was once again in the ring against George. Ali wanted to become the first man in history to put George on the canvas. He didn't make a dent. The fight

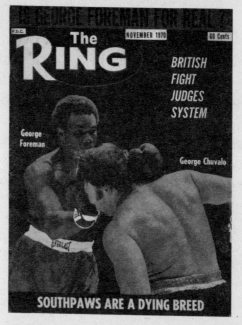

It was like George Foreman was flattening Chuvalo's face with every punch. Foreman would eventually become the heavyweight champion of the world.

went the full ten rounds and George was never knocked down. Ali won, but George's reputation lived on. George made $65,000 for fighting Ali a second time.

Memorable Ali Fights

- Fight of the Century — Ali vs. Frazier, March 8, 1971: Most anticipated fight of all time because both fighters were undefeated. It became Ali's first professional loss.
- Rumble in the Jungle — Ali vs. Foreman, October 30, 1974: Bout took place in Kinshasa, Zaire. Ali won back the World title.
- Thrilla in Manila — Ali vs. Frazier, October 1, 1975: Third fight between the two fighters. Ali kept the title.

By 1972 George was 34 years old. The time between his fights was getting longer and longer. But he had finally reached the level where he made lot of money. In eight years under Ungerman's management, George earned more than $500,000.

George's success in the ring allowed him to become a businessman. He used his winnings to earn more money out of the ring. Along with Ungerman, George was a success in areas like real estate. In the past he had always worried about his financial future. It looked like he never had to worry again.

By 1973 George's interest in boxing was fading. He turned his focus to his family and non-boxing activities. It looked like he would never return.

14 Still Standing

As George fought less and less, his star went dim in the public eye. People didn't ask him for autographs as much as they did when he still had a chance at the World title. He knew that time had run out on any chance to reverse history.

But leaving the ring was not a simple decision for George. Even though he was doing well outside the ring, he felt the pull to climb back into it.

"Life gets boring sometimes," said

George to the *Star*. "At least when you're fighting there's a little action, something to live for, something to get fired up about."

In 1975, the 38-year-old was stripped of his Canadian title. The Canadian Professional Boxing Federation (CPBF)

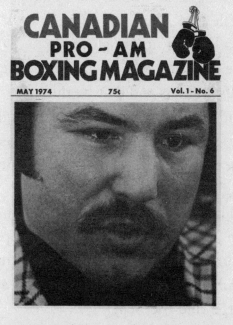

George was not the slim boxer he once was, but he could still pack a punch.

thought he hadn't defended it enough.

It was a major blow to the longtime champ. He made plans to regain the title.

"One more fight," George told the *Star* on his return to the ring in 1977. "I'm going to clear the whole thing up, then I'm going to say goodbye. I'm going to get the title back, then I'm going to look for a wall and hang up my gloves."

He admitted that his face had taken on a puffy softness and that he might be a few pounds overweight. He hadn't fought in three years. But, at 39 years of age, he wanted to be the champ again. He still thought he was the best in Canada.

"The real reason I want to fight once more is that all the other chumps are coming along and talking about the Canadian title. I'd hate to just kiss it away," George told the *Star*.

George would fight Bob Felstein for the vacant Canadian title. Like George,

Felstein was an aging fighter who had seen better days. People wondered if the fighters would even show up, would land a single punch, or die of a heart attack due to their ages. Five thousand people attended the fight to see what would happen.

George, overflowing from his trunks, knocked Felstein out in the ninth round. Chuvalo was once again Canadian champ. He decided to continue fighting and defending the title.

"Chuvalo never again will fight the big fight, but he's a big fish in a very small Canadian pond. There is nobody on the horizon who can beat him," wrote the *Star*. "He enjoys being somewhat of a legend in his own time. The legend of indestructibility. In his career he has knocked out 64 opponents, won 9 decisions, suffered 18 losses, and had 2 draws."

Chuvalo's 93rd career fight was against George Jerome. He won in two rounds.

His next fight wasn't in the ring as he had hoped. He would fight the CPBF and its president Ron Hazter. They told George to fight Trevor Berbrick by February 27, 1979, or lose the title.

Berbrick wanted the fight in Halifax.

The End of the Greatest Career

Originally from Jamaica, Trevor Berbrick competed in the 1976 Olympics in Montreal. He decided to stay in Canada. He will always be known as the boxer who ended Muhammad Ali's career. He defeated the 39-year-old Ali by unanimous decision in 1981. Ali never fought again. Ali was officially diagnosed with Parkinson's Syndrome in 1984. It's an illness that takes over the body so a person cannot control themselves. Ali's boxing record was 56-5.

George wanted it in Toronto. The champ should have had the choice of venue. They couldn't work out the details. The CPBF stripped the title from George.

"For the past 21 years I have been the heavyweight champion," George told the *Star*. "Two days ago a man named Ron Hazter took away my pride and championship with a telegram. I earned that championship by fighting for myself, my family, and Canada."

George lost his fight against the CPBF. He would never regain the Canadian title. He also would never be in another pro fight. In 93 career pro fights, George had a record of 73 wins, 18 losses, and 2 draws.

Once he retired, George started appearing in TV commercials and had small parts in movies. The high point was his own TV show, *George Chuvalo Presents Famous Knockouts*.

George tried to stay connected to the

boxing world. He trained, managed, and promoted boxing in Toronto. He said that when you are promoting a fight, "you're in the action. There's a fight coming up. It's the same kind of feeling as when you're fighting — am I going to make it or not."

Sadly, George would never be the success in someone else's corner as he had been inside the ring. To George's dismay, his boxers failed to work as hard as he had.

George finally cut his ties to boxing. He put his efforts in other ventures. He would also have to put his attention to events taking place under his own roof.

15 *The Hardest Fight*

George's professional boxing career lasted more than 20 years. He was always there, always ready to fight all comers. There was no one like him then, and there has been no one like him since.

George Chuvalo became a Canadian legend. He was the man not even the great Muhammad Ali could topple. But rising to that level put him in the spotlight for everyone to see. For most of his life he was known as the boxer. His children were known for their whole lives as a boxer's kids. Even after George retired, his sons felt that pressure.

They had high expectations placed on them. People thought they should be great fighters like their father. They were challenged on the schoolyard, on the streets, and when they played sports.

"My father worked at Canada Packers. My kids were George Chuvalo's kids. I was Steven Chuvalo's son — he was a butcher. It's very different," said George, who never wanted his sons to be boxers.

Instead of boxing, George's sons Mitch, Jesse, Stephen, and George Lee played hockey. In high school George's oldest son Mitch became a football star. After graduation he earned a scholarship to play football at Florida State University. He would grow up to become a well-respected teacher in the Toronto area.

But the lives of George's other three

Celebrating Chuvalo

After retiring from boxing, George Chuvalo was inducted into the Canadian Sports Hall of Fame, was made a member of the Order of Canada, and was given a star on Canada's Walk of Fame.

sons wouldn't turn out as well.

As young adults Jesse, Stephen, and George Lee started using drugs. They all became addicts. And their father seemed to be the last one to see what was going on.

"If I knew what was happening to Jesse that would have been my number one priority. But I wasn't aware of it," said George in an interview with Stephen Brunt. "Even when I found out he was using I somehow thought he'd quit. You'll be all right. You're a tough kid."

On February 18, 1985, only nine months after he first got into drugs, Jesse went into his bedroom and shot himself. He was 20 years old.

The death of a child is never easy. The man who never went down in 93 fights was stopped cold.

"It's like everything you breathe in is grief and you can't believe your son has died," said George in a CBC interview. "The ache and that sense of loss will always be with me. I lost my son in the cruellest way possible. Suicide is the cruellest thing that can happen. Anyone who loses a son feels that they have failed somewhere."

Steven and George Lee used drugs even more after Jesse's death. They were hooked on drugs and would do anything to buy more. They even sold their father's Canadian Amateur Heavyweight Championship medal to buy drugs.

George tried to get them clean, but nothing worked.

Steven and George Lee turned to crime to feed their addictions. They were caught and were sentenced to jail time. George's sons were clean in jail. He hoped they wouldn't return to drugs when they were released.

Four days after getting out of jail, George Lee was found dead in a seedy Toronto hotel. He had died from a drug overdose.

Two days after George buried his son, he found his wife Lynne dead. She had killed herself. After losing another son she felt she couldn't go on living.

The shock of his wife's death sent George down for the count.

"They say I was in bed for a month and a half," said George in a *Macleans* magazine interview. "After that friends would come around, my family, but I don't remember. I must have got out of bed to go to the bathroom, but I don't remember."

George had nothing to focus on but to save Steven. He vowed not to bury a third son. But in 1995 Steven was arrested and charged for another crime. He went back to jail.

Once again, Steven was forced to kick the habit while in jail. When he got out, it was supposed to be a clean start to a new life. He even planned to talk about the dangers of drugs at his brother Mitch's school.

Two weeks after his release from jail, Steven lost his fight against drugs. On August 17, 1996, Steven died of a drug overdose.

While growing up, George Chuvalo had dreamed of becoming the heavyweight champion of the world. His life was centred by that one goal. Now George had a new focus in life. He would fight against the drugs that had taken much of his family from him.

Epilogue

George Chuvalo was known as a tough fighter who couldn't be knocked off his feet. The death of three sons and his wife was almost enough to knock him down. He was still standing because he still had a lot to live for. This included a son, a daughter, grandchildren, and new wife Joanne.

"I'm lucky because I'm surrounded by people who care for me. I have some good friends. If it wasn't for my friends and my beautiful remaining family I wouldn't be here," George said in an interview with Barry Lindenman. "Nobody can survive without love. That's the one thing that keeps me motivated to do anything."

Tragic events pushed George's life in a new direction. He set out on a mission to describe how drugs took his family from him. He decided to travel across the

George Chuvalo went across Canada to give his message about drug abuse. Here he is talking to a school class.

country to spread his message about drugs. He has started his own organization, George Chuvalo's Fight Against Drugs.

Instead of going to the gym, he went to schools, jails, and drug treatment centres.

George gives people something to think about. He describes in detail how his sons became drug addicts and lost their lives. He talks about how drugs ripped his family apart and the pain of burying his wife and three sons.

He speaks to high-school students because they are at the crossroads of their lives. "They don't know the potential devastating effect of drugs," George says. "I feel that explaining my story in graphic detail will show them that drugs aren't the way to go and that drug abuse could easily happen to them."

George Chuvalo's Fight Against Drugs has become George's purpose. It is a fight he might not always win. But he was willing to go the distance again to make a difference.

Glossary

Amateur: An athlete who is not paid.

Bout: A boxing match that has one-minute breaks between a set number of rounds.

Card/Fight card: All of the boxing matches that occur during an evening of a boxing event are on the fight card. The main event is the most important fight on the card. Popular fighters box in the main event. The undercard fights have less-popular fighters.

Championship: A competition, or contest, for a title or prize.

Clinch: When a boxer clutches an opponent to avoid being punched.

Combination: A series of punches thrown in sequence; e.g., a left jab, followed by a straight right punch, followed by a left hook.

Count: Number of seconds the referee counts after a boxer is knocked down.

Down for the count: A boxer who is knocked down for the count of ten.

Draw: A tie that is the result of opponents scoring the same number of points.

Fouls: Actions by a boxer that the referee doesn't feel meet the standard of a fair blow, or is unsportsmanlike conduct.

Going the distance: A boxer's ability to make it through all the scheduled rounds.

Hook: A sideways punch done with the arm bent like a hook.

Jab: A quick, sharp punch that shoots out from chin level.

Knocked down: When a boxer touches the ground with anything other than his or her feet, or is being held up by the ropes.

Knockout: When a knocked-down boxer does not rise by the count of ten.

Left hook: A hook with the left fist.

Manager: A person who gets paid to act as the boxer's agent or representative.

Match: A contest between two boxers.

Opponent: The rival boxer, player, or team.

Prizefighter: A boxer who fights for money.

Professional: A person who is paid to work as an athlete.

Punching bag: Punching bags are bags commonly used in boxing training. A *heavy bag* is a large, firm, cylindrical-shaped bag filled with sand or cloth rags. It hangs from the ceiling by chains or rope. It is used to practice powerful body punches. A *speed bag* is a small, air-filled, teardrop-shaped leather bag. It is hung from the ceiling at eye level. Hitting it improves a boxer's hand-eye coordination, speed, arm strength, and endurance.

Purse: The money a boxer gets for winning a fight.

Record: A boxing record shows how successful a boxer has been. It compares a boxer's wins-losses-draws. Records are also used to compare boxers to each other. The better boxer should have more wins and less losses.

Referee: An official who makes sure that the rules of sport are followed.

Round: A three-minute period when boxers fight in the ring.

Title: A title can be won or lost. The boxer who holds the title is called the champion. A boxer who wants to win the title is called a contender. A contender wins the title if they defeat the champion.

Unanimous decision: When all three judges agree on a winner.

Uppercut: An upward punch delivered at close range.

Acknowledgements

For me, the most exciting part of writing a history book is researching. It involves finding out everything I can possibly learn about the subject. With technology this has gotten easier.

I started my research in various online newspaper archives. I searched through 50 years of *Toronto Star*, *Globe and Mail*, and *New York Times* newspapers. I got to follow George from a young fighter through to his retirement.

The CBC Digital Archives held a section devoted to George Chuvalo. It was called *Still Standing: The People's Champion George Chuvalo*. This archive held seven radio and fourteen television clips. There was over 300 minutes of recorded information about George.

The website Cyber Boxing Zone had a great interview with George conducted by Barry Lindenman. It also had a database of all his fight results.

An important look into George's life was a documentary movie called *The Last Round: The Untold Story of the Fighter who took Muhammad Ali the Distance* directed by Joseph Blasioli. It is a documentary about George's life before his first fight against Ali in 1966. It gave me a greater understanding of George's career up to that point. The interviews with journalists in the film helped me create the story surrounding George's fights against Ali, Terrell, and Patterson.

Globe and Mail journalist Stephen Brunt is a great resource for anything George Chuvalo. His interviews with George are important because they brought out interesting feelings about his career and family. Brunt's book *Facing Ali* gave me information about Ali's career and opponents. It also contained great

information about George's life and his fight against Ali. All George Chuvalo quotes used in the book have come from Brunt interviews and the other media sources listed above.

On a personal note, I would like to thank friends and family for all their support. I would especially like to thank my wife, Shelley. She was always there to pick me up when I was down.

Lastly, I would like to thank the people at James Lorimer and Company. Thank you for letting me write for the Recordbooks Series. And, thank you to my editor Faye Smailes for her guidance in writing this book.

About the Author

Richard Brignall is a journalist from Kenora, Ontario, who writes for *Cottage Life* and *Outdoor Canada*. He was previously the sports reporter for the *Kenora Daily Miner and News*. He is the author of the Recordbooks volumes *Forever Champions*, *Small Town Glory* with co-author, with John Danakas.

Photo Credits

We gratefully acknowledge the following sources for permission to reproduce the images in this book.

City of Toronto Archives: p 20: Series 1047, Item 2470; p 74 and back cover (middle): Series 306, Sub-Series 5, File 10, id002; p 135: Series 306, Sub-Series 5, File 10, id001

Library and Archives Canada: p 81, front cover (top)

Milton Historical Society: p 148 (originally from "The Canadian Champion")

Sports and Entertainment Publications (Ring Magazine): p 78, p 120, p 131, back cover (bottom)

Other images supplied by the author

Index

punches, types of, 30